CAROL BURNETT

A Little Golden Book® Biography

By Andrea Posner-Sanc

Illustrated by Kelly Kennedy

A GOLDEN BOOK • NEW YORK

 Published in the United States by Golden Books, an imprint of Random House Children's Books, a division of Penguin Random House LLC, 1745 Broadway, New York, NY 10019. Golden Books, A Golden Book, A Little Golden Book, the G colophon, and the distinctive gold spine are registered trademarks of Penguin Random House LLC.
rhcbooks.com
Educators and librarians, for a variety of teaching tools, visit us at RHTeachersLibrarians.com
Library of Congress Control Number: 2022931978
ISBN 978-0-593-48191-2 (trade) — ISBN 978-0-593-48192-9 (ebook)
Printed in the United States of America
10 9 8 7 6 5 4 3 2 1

Carol Creighton Burnett was born in San Antonio, Texas, on April 26, 1933. Her parents, Joseph and Ina Louise, loved her very much, but they decided it would be best for her to be raised by her grandmother. Carol called her Nanny.

When Carol was seven years old, she and Nanny moved to Hollywood, California. Lots of wealthy movie stars lived and worked in Hollywood.

But Carol and Nanny were poor. They lived in a tiny one-room apartment with a Murphy bed, a bed that is pulled down from the wall at night and lifted up and hidden during the day. Nanny slept on the bed, and Carol slept on the couch.

Nanny and Carol liked to go to the movies as often as possible. Sometimes they saw eight movies a week! Back then, Carol's ticket cost just ten cents.

After seeing a movie, Carol would act out the scenes with friends on the roof of her apartment building. She started dreaming of being an actress and having her own happy ending, just like in the movies.

After high school, Carol studied theater arts at the University of California in Los Angeles, where she performed in many shows. She loved being in front of an audience. And more than anything, Carol wanted to be in a Broadway musical.

A stranger who had seen Carol perform helped her get closer to that dream. He gave her a thousand dollars to move to New York. But she had to promise to pay him back in five years, to help others if she became successful, and to never tell anyone his name. Carol agreed.

Moving away from Nanny was hard, but Carol was excited about her future.

In New York City, she lived in a room with four other women who also hoped to get into show business. When she wasn't going on auditions, she worked as a hatcheck girl in a restaurant. Carol earned a quarter whenever a customer left their hat or shopping bags with her before sitting down to eat.

Carol learned that she needed an agent in order to get cast in a show. But the agents wanted to see her perform before they agreed to work with her. So what did Carol do? She wrote her own show with her roommates and invited all the agents to come see them. It worked—Carol got an agent!

She soon got a part on a children's TV show. When she called Nanny to tell her the good news, Nanny asked Carol to say hello to her during the show. That wasn't possible, so instead, she gave her left ear a tug. It was a secret signal to Nanny, letting her know that she loved her.

Even though Nanny died in 1967, Carol has continued to pull on her ear every time she's on television.

Carol's big break came when she joined *The Garry Moore Show.* She played many characters in many different skits in this popular variety show. Her natural talent and her silly faces made her a favorite with audiences.

At the same time, Carol was cast as the lead in a Broadway musical. Her dream had come true! Carol played Princess Winnifred the Woebegone in *Once Upon a Mattress*—a show based on the fairy tale "The Princess and the Pea."

She worked at the TV show during the day and performed in the musical at night. It was exhausting. She once fell asleep onstage, on top of twenty mattresses. The stage manager had to wake her up to say her lines!

Carol and the show were a hit. She was able to pay back the thousand dollars she had borrowed from the kind stranger exactly five years after she had received it.

In 1963, Carol and her husband, Joe Hamilton, welcomed a baby daughter they named Carrie. A couple of years later, they moved to Los Angeles. They went on to have two more daughters, Jody and Erin, to complete their family.

Carol was a great mom. She loved playing board games and watching old movie musicals with her girls.

When Carol was offered the chance to star in her own TV series, she chose to do a variety show. After all, it was what she knew—and liked—best. But no woman had ever hosted such a show. Would anyone watch? You bet they would!

The Carol Burnett Show began airing in 1967. It ran for eleven seasons and won twenty-five Emmy Awards.

Every show began with Carol taking questions from the audience. Actors on other shows talked with their audiences, too, but Carol was the first to tape these chats and show them on TV. They helped her fans feel as if they really knew her. And Carol loved how surprising the questions could be. Once, a woman asked Carol where the bathroom was!

Her costars Harvey Korman, Vicki Lawrence, Lyle Waggoner, and Tim Conway helped add to the fun. Sometimes they surprised one another by improvising—making up lines instead of following the script. Many of the show's funniest moments came when Carol and the others couldn't help laughing in the middle of a scene.

Some of Carol's favorite skits made fun of the old movies she and Nanny had watched together. In one, Carol's character makes a dress from the curtains in her home—and includes the curtain rod!

This costume is so famous, it is part of the collection of the National Museum of American History in Washington, DC.

In 2005, President George W. Bush presented Carol with the Presidential Medal of Freedom. And in 2019, she received a special Golden Globe named for her: The Carol Burnett Award. Every year since, this award has been given to someone who has done remarkable work in television, just like Carol.

Carol has spent her career playing hundreds of different characters, but she has also shared her true self with her audiences. And as she promised to the stranger who'd believed in her so many years ago, she has helped many people with her generosity and support.

Each episode of *The Carol Burnett Show* ended with her singing "I'm So Glad We Had This Time Together"—and Carol's fans feel the very same way.